WHY *You* MATTER

WHY *You* MATTER

BECOMING A *Daughter* OF VALOR

KIMBERLY L. HIGDON

Xulon Press

Xulon Press
2301 Lucien Way #415
Maitland, FL 32751
407.339.4217
www.xulonpress.com

Paperback ISBN-13: 978-1-66285-606-8

Ebook ISBN-13: 978-1-66285-607-5

Contents

Introduction

L ife is not meant to be an easygoing journey with the intention of arriving safely at heaven's door in a well-maintained, preserved body. It is more likely for us to get there skidding in sideways, totally worn-out, praising God because we made it, saying, "Woo-hoo, Father, what a ride." Romans 8:28 says, "And we know that all things work together for good to them that love God, to them who are the called according to *his* purpose." If we already know all things work together—whether they're good, bad, painful, lonely, or even happy, loving times—and all these things work together for good, then why do we have such a hard time accepting the negative experiences of life? But God, who is rich in mercy with His great love, loved us first. Get that: *first*. He loved us first, even when we were dead in our sins. God, through His grace and mercy, enlightened us by taking our sins and bringing us full circle, joining us with Christ to shine more brightly and live life freely. Nothing that you or I have done could earn this grace, nor do we deserve it. God has raised us up together. Here is the key word: *together*. For we are God's workmanship, created in Christ Jesus for good works that God prepared ahead of time for you and me to do.

Chapter 1

Changing Your Mindset

S o where am I going with this? I want to talk to you
about the way we think, our mindset. When we go
through things in life that are upsetting and downright
hard, God is wanting us to realize He is allowing these
times to mold us and change our attitude to be more like
Christ. Did you know there is nothing we go through here
on earth that Christ Jesus, *himself*, didn't face while He
was here too? We all go through hardships. They are a
part of life. It rains on the just as it does the unjust. God
reminds us in John 16:33 that we will go through trials
here, and we can either choose to let these moments in
life affect us for the better or infect us for the worse.

It's kind of like a wound. If you don't choose to take
care of it, it will cause you pain and suffering over time.
Even when it finally scabs over, if you pick at it, it can
bleed and fester, swelling up, and become infected. This is
just like the hard circumstances of life. If we look at them
through our own eyes, they can affect us and our attitudes,
making us feel angry, even depressed—not only affecting
us but those around us too. So many times, when life gets
hard and our burdens are heavy, we can be brought low.
At times we tend not to lean on the Lord because we feel

like He is punishing us or doesn't love us. Instead of letting these hard times draw us close to Him, we allow them to push us away from Him. We allow our thoughts of them to infect us, causing us to be weary and feel worthless and of no value anymore.

This is not what God wants for us in these moments of life. He wants us to think as Christ thought. In Philippians 2 God tells us to adopt the same mindset, the same attitude of Christ Jesus. This is where working together comes into play. Our mindset should be that of Christ—the way we think of ourselves, our life, our surroundings, our world, and those within our realm of influence. What do they see when they see us? What are you and I portraying to those around us? Is it confusion, doubt, worry, fear, even instability? James 1:8 tells us that when we are double-minded, we don't think or act right and we are unstable in all our ways. Kind of like the ocean waves tossing back and forth, back and forth on the beach. Think about it: What do you want them to see? Do you want them to see someone who is rich in mercy, who loves others without comparison, and who is caring and a joy to be around? Or someone who when others see you coming, they want to go the other way because of the uncertainty of who you are today, like Dr. Jekyll or Mr. Hyde? 1 Samuel 16:7 *paraphrased* states, "Man looks on the outside, but God looks at the heart."

We all want to be taken seriously for who we truly are, not for who others say we are. What someone says about you or me, their opinion, does not have to be our reality. For me to live is Christ and to die is gain. Do you and I really live our lives like this? As I sit here writing, the author who comes to mind whom I truly enjoy is Max Lucado. But God has created and gifted me to be who He created me to be, just like He has gifted you to be the *you*

He created you to be. My prayer for you as you read this book is for God to change your perspective, your thought life, about what you've been through, about what you live in, and about what is to come in your life while you're here. He has done this for me, and I know He will do the same for you.

May we all rise to this moment to be the one and only true exceptionally unique individual God created us to be. God wants to reset our minds, refocusing us on who we really are and how special we truly are to Him. We are here at this appointed time in our life for a purpose. God has given each of us a platform to be used to bring Him honor and glory, working together with Him for His kingdom purpose. Now is the time. Jesus wants you and me to be contagiously courageous and brave, which is how God has created us to be. This all begins with changing your viewpoint and your mindset about yourself. Let's dive in and see what God has in store for you on why you matter.

Now, here's a word: *puzzled*. I know you're possibly thinking, "Puzzled?" But let's look at it for just a moment. Things in life sure can be puzzling. Take, for instance, a puzzle. How do you view or work a puzzle? Puzzles come in all different shapes and sizes—some big, some small, some round, some square. Even the number of pieces and themes and colors vary. The characteristics are so different, but yet they all have one thing in common: they have to be put together. Think for a moment: How do you work a puzzle? Do you do the outside first to frame in your edges and see just how big this puzzle is going to be? Or do you sort through the pieces, finding different shapes and colors, picking out the ones that are similar and categorizing them to get started? Maybe you just dump the whole puzzle out, sort through the pieces, and work similar sections, then link them together. There really is no right or wrong way to work a puzzle. However, it is best, through the process, to look at the picture and view what the final product should look like. Could you even imagine there not being a picture to look at?

Our lives can be compared to that of a puzzle. Just like a puzzle, none of the pieces are the same. They may be similar in size, shape, and even color. They may even seem to fit in more than one place, but none of them are alike. They all have their place to be. Just like the circumstances in our lives, each piece/season of our lives can be like a part of the bigger picture. Or even yet, each piece/season can represent you and me as being a part of this thing called life. Just like a puzzle piece, none of us are the same. We all have some similarities, such as physical traits—a mouth to eat and talk with and eyes to see, for example. But God fashioned you and me individually and uniquely. Just like a piece of puzzle that's fashioned by the designer, but must be put together to see the whole picture. We too must work together to see this whole picture called life.

You and I may style our hair the same way or we may even like the same kind of dessert, but we are all still unique. We may even have the same favorite color. Mine changes from time to time because I really like them all, but if I had to choose just one, it would have to be purple. What color would you choose? These are examples of where we might be the same, but just like puzzle pieces, we come in all different shapes, sizes, and colors, and that's okay.

The world likes to try to make us fit into a mold of what we should be, how we should look, and how we should act, but we all are created wonderfully and beautifully different. In a puzzle, each piece must be examined and taken note of to see where it goes and then put in its proper place to fit. God, in His perfect plan, made all of us different just like the designer of a puzzle did. God created you and me for a purpose, and from His point of view, He sees the whole picture of each of our lives.

Just think, before you were ever formed in your mother's womb, God had a plan, a purpose for creating you as the unique *you* that you are. In Psalms 139:16 God tells you and me that before we were ever thought of by our parents, when we were formless, He already knew us and had a plan for us, something to do here on earth right at this very moment in time. No matter what the circumstances were that surrounded you being here, when you were conceived or how you came to be, you are here now intentionally on purpose. God doesn't make any mistakes. Therefore, you and me being here is no mistake. Just like the cliché "God doesn't make junk," so neither you nor I are junk. We were created to be here. Just like the pieces of a puzzle. They have a purpose in their design, and so do you and I. It is meant for us to be here working together.

That being said, it's such encouragement to know we don't have to do it all by ourselves. God doesn't intend for us to be alone and doing life alone. Satan likes to make us think we don't belong here, keeping us in a vicious cycle of feeling we're too messed up or not intelligent enough to do what God has created us to do. Satan likes to keep us bogged down in our thoughts so that we stay focused on our inadequacies and our struggles, the lies that he feeds us. He does it to all of us. Satan makes us feel singled out, like we're the only one going through the hard, difficult times, but God tells us in John 8:44 that Satan is a liar and the father of all lies. Satan cannot speak truth because there is no truth in him. He likes to keep us so wrapped up in the cares of this world, reminding us of our past failures and mistakes, causing us to compare ourselves to others, and overwhelming us with feelings of loneliness to give into these ever-changing emotions that we all have.

Satan is crafty like that and not creative like God. God promises us that we will have troubles here in this world (1 Peter 4:12-13). God created you and He knows each one of us so personally and completely. Did you know when He sees us, He sees us as equal? From His point of view, He sees where the blood has been applied and where it hasn't. He doesn't see us as the world sees us, and neither should we. When we look at each other through the lens of this world, we tend to compare ourselves one with another. We become more focused on ourselves and less focused on what God wants us to be. Sure, we all want to be liked and fit in with those around us, but are we portraying Jesus to those who need Him as their Savior? Are we portraying Him to those who are in our realm of influence? Or are we portraying someone who doesn't know where to go or what to trust in? Someone who is always trying to better themselves, trying to fit in and do things themselves instead of trusting and leaning on Jesus? Just think about it: Jesus came and took our past, present, and future sins and placed them upon Himself for each and every one of us so that we could live in freedom. In spite of this, we continue to live in bondage, bound down by the cares of this world. We forget who we really are in Jesus. Jesus paid the price for our bondage and shed His blood for all of us so that we could live in freedom. So why do we act as if we're still in chains? Why are we so wrapped up in our thoughts and our failures thinking we have no value or worth? Some of it is this world and its ideal of what we should be and what we should live up to, but then some of it is our own thought process of thinking negatively. Satan keeps us so wrapped up in all these things that it robs us of our peace and joy. When this happens, we can't be the unique individuals God created us to be here on earth. With that being said, how can we change our perspective, our mental thoughts of these things, and think from heaven's point of view about our lives and others'?

We all have had things in our lives, or still do, that can harden us in our thoughts of ourselves. God doesn't allow these things to happen to us in life to harden us or cause us to think less of ourselves; He just wants to use them to mold us into His image to be more like Him. Remember, life's disappointments are God's appointments; they are really meant to be like bridges and not dams in our lives. They are not our enemies to weigh us down or drown us. They are lessons in life to help us be overcomers, not to halt us in our tracks and build walls around us and not let anyone else in. This would be a prison sentence for you or me to live in. God doesn't want us to dwell on these things either. He wants us to have peace that passes all understanding as spoken of in Philippians 4:7.

I have bridges in my own life that I have had to cross and some bridges that God is still working with me on. Do you have bridges you must cross too? They don't have to define us. God wants to use us not in spite of these bridges, but because of them. These battle scars and wounds can be used for His glory. It's all about what you and I believe about these things in our life. Just think how much more meaningful our life could be if we would allow God to heal us through changing the way we view and endure these challenging situations God allows us to go through. It's all about our mindset and the way we perceive them.

Let's talk about the way we stereotype throughout our life. According to Webster's dictionary, stereotyping is believing unfairly that all people or things with a certain characteristic or attribute are the same. So many times, we are either stereotyped by someone or we stereotype each other, or we're guilty of stereotyping other groups of people. This is what the world does, and boy that's like the blind leading the blind.

I'm reminded of back in the day when my husband was in the U.S. Air Force and we were stationed in Grand Forks, North Dakota. Grand Forks was a little town just south of the border of Manitoba, Canada. The weather is so cold most of the time there, with only approximately two months max of summer heat. In the cold months, we would head to the mall for entertainment. Now, I don't know where you are from, but the mall back then had only a few stores. Sometimes our entertainment was to grab a Coke—or *pop*, as they would say—and we would sit on the bench and just people-watch.

Have you ever just sat and watched people? If so, what did you notice about them? Is it the way they styled their hair or the way they talked and walked? Maybe it was the way they dressed or who they were associated with? Maybe even better yet, the family they were with? What are the things you notice when you look at people? I ask these questions because of the thoughts that we all have about others. Maybe we stereotype because of the way we grew up or even by the standard of the school we went to. How about even the car we drive or the house we live in? The list can go on and on. Have you ever thought about how Jesus, when He walked here on earth, chose the twelve disciples? Jesus didn't choose them because of the way they looked but because He saw their hearts.

Think: How do we even remember the twelve disciples today? Can you name the twelve disciples and where they are mentioned? I sometimes wonder if all the disciples had known just how we would remember them, if they would even have carried on.

Let's take a look at some of these twelve disciples Jesus chose. Andrew, the first to be chosen of the twelve, was also known as Simon Peter's brother. Question here: Do you have a brother or sister, and if so, what if you were only known by your sibling whenever your name was mentioned? What would others think or say about you? Another disciple was Thomas. Thomas was known as the Doubter! Why? Because he doubted that Jesus was who He said He was. Thomas wanted to see and touch the nail prints in Jesus's hands before he would believe Jesus had truly risen (John 20:24–29).

If someone pinned a character trait on you, what would it be? What would you be known for? I'm not sure what others would say about me, but just recently I was attacked by a swarm of bees and had to have surgery on my right foot due to jumping off an embankment to get away from them. On the second visit to the doctor after having surgery, he said, "Oh no, I can already tell you're timid." That's a story for another time, but some might call me timid. How about the two brothers, James and John, who Jesus called "Boanerges," which means "Sons of Thunder," mentioned in Mark 3:17? Were they called this possibly because of their tempers? In the recordings of Luke, they were willing to call fire down from heaven and kill the Samaritans who rejected Jesus (Luke 9:54). Did you know that John called himself the disciple who Jesus loved? It is recorded only in the Gospel of John that he penned himself.

How about Peter? Simon Peter, called Cephas, which interpreted means "Rock." He was the disciple who walked on water but then took his eyes off Jesus and started to sink. Peter also lost his temper, took a sword, and cut off the ear of the high priest's servant, Malchus. He even denied he was associated with Jesus and that he was a disciple, not just once but three times the night Jesus was taken (Luke 22:54–62). Jesus had just forewarned Peter and the disciples in verse 31 that Satan had already asked if he could sift them like wheat. In spite of the warning from Jesus, Peter still denied him. A lot of people, myself included, have compared themselves to Peter because Peter is known throughout the Bible to speak before thinking, for opening a can of worms, and for all his failures.

Then there's Matthew—sweet, innocent Matthew— also known as Levi, who was a tax collector, and nobody liked him because he was always taking their money. He just longed to be accepted and loved.

So what do we know of these disciples now? Andrew: his brother's sibling, Thomas the Doubter. James and John: Sons of Thunder. Peter: the one known for opening his mouth and speaking before thinking. And Matthew: the one nobody liked. In spite of what we know of them, what if they had not kept going? Where would you and I be right now? Better yet where would our families be? Would there be any churches here that preach the truth about the Gospel of Jesus Christ? God had them here in history and on earth at their appointed time for a purpose just like He has you and me here now in our appointed time of purpose. The things we tend to forget about these disciples is what actually mattered. They gave up their lives to follow Jesus. What others thought of them and what we think of them does not define them. The things they did or didn't do, or even what they experienced, did not define them. Neither does what we do or don't do define us. When we accept Jesus as our Savior, we too are to be Jesus's personal disciples. These disciples were no different than you or I. They too had their similarities but also differences, faults, failures, and shortcomings. Did you know that none of them were scholars either? Jesus met them right where they were, and they answered the call to follow Him and did just that: followed Him. Think about it: they left their families, gave up friends, left their jobs and homes behind to answer Jesus's call. These ordinary disciples were just like us, and they did extraordinary things for God. Yet we tend to mostly remember them for their hang-ups, downfalls, and failures of their lives and not for the great missions they accomplished. They finished well and furthered the Gospel for Jesus Christ in spite of what others thought or said about them.

Andrew actually brought his brother Peter to Jesus. After Pentecost, Andrew became a missionary and preached the Gospel until he was martyred for his faith. Peter became a fiery, fearless missionary for Jesus and spread the Gospel throughout Rome. He also wrote 1st Peter and 2nd Peter. James was the brother of John, and he proclaimed the Gospel after Jesus's resurrection. James was the first disciple to be martyred because of his faith in Jesus. John, James's younger brother, preached the love of Jesus, writing the book of John; 1st, 2nd, and 3rd John; and Revelation. John lived in exile on the island called Patmos, where he wrote Revelation and was said to have died of natural causes. Matthew went on to write the book of Matthew and he spread the Gospel in Ethiopia until he was possibly martyred for his faith in Jesus too. They all went on to be founders of the modern churches in spreading the furtherance of the Good News, the Gospel of Jesus Christ. Through the disciples' hard work, living life through persecutions, tribulations, trials, many sorrows, sufferings, and hardships, they formed the foundation for the Christian church, initiating the movement that has steadily spread across the world even to where you and I live today. The disciples represented their Lord and Master Jesus Christ, and He chose them to represent His name as one single entity, one identity, in spite of all their differences. Each disciple took care of what Jesus asked them to do with the same vision and same goal in mind: to reach others for Jesus, to move forward and succeed in the spread of the Good News, the true Gospel.

So many times we tend to judge someone by what we hear or think, just like we have these disciples. We judge someone by how they portray themselves and don't take to heart who they really are. Do you realize this is exactly how Satan and this world we live in want us to be? They want us to focus on the bad and the negatives about someone because it makes us feel better and look better ourselves. We even have pity on certain people looking down on them or just having nothing to do with them at all. Neither you nor I know what is in someone's life, what they've been through, or what they may be going through that has affected them. Better yet, do you or I even know what each other has lived through in life that has affected us or infected us, portraying us how we are seen today?

No wonder this world is so full of people who are having a problem with their identity. Are you one of those individuals who has had, or has, a problem with your identity? I would have to answer yes to this question because I have had a problem with my identity. This leads me to my next thought: your identity.

Do you know your true identity? If you have accepted Jesus as your personal Savior, then you are a child of God. Do you know what it means to be a child of God? Each and every one of our lives is like a book. People are trying to read you and me all the time. Have you ever stopped to think about the fact that when someone passes away, it's like a book has died right along with them? I can't help but think of my hairdresser who died a couple of years ago. When we moved a little more than five years ago, it took me a while to find a hairdresser, and I was so excited when I finally found someone who did my hair the way I liked it. She would share with me her knowledge of color and what it does to skin undertones and how color makes a person's eyes look brighter and brings them to life. I couldn't help but think when this individual was killed that the knowledge and wisdom she had died right along with her. All those years of schooling and learning, the time spent was gone with her just like that.

Life truly is short. God tells us life is but a vapor and we're not even promised a tomorrow (James 4:14). Think of a vapor; it is always fleeting—here one second and gone in the next. Life is like that. Some of us live as if our life is a closed book, one that lays on a shelf waiting to be given a chance to be read. But some of us live life as if we're an open book for all to see. This could be by your own choosing or maybe because of your family. Maybe your family held a prominent position in the eyes of the public or something of that sort. No matter how you live your life, you cannot live above the stereotyping of what people are going to say or think about you. I don't know how you grew up, but I grew up being around church people. As some people call it, I was churched all my life. From what I was told, I was even in church for the nine months of my life in my mother's womb.

Chapter 2

Growing Up in Ministry

Throughout my lifetime, my dad always has been in some kind of ministry, and most of that has been pastoring. I can actually say my siblings and I were drugged children. We were drug here and drug there, just about anywhere there was something going on for a church function. I want to say right up front: I am very grateful for my heritage of Jesus and being raised in church. I have very fond memories of my childhood, and I wouldn't have that part of my life any other way. Now that I'm older and more mature in the Lord, I can look back and be more grateful than I was then for His grace and mercy. Through it all, His provisions, and the way He has protected me from things that God only knows about, is something I will forever be thankful for. I grew up around many different people. Sometimes these people were closer than my own family. So many precious saints of God I cherish have been a part of my life.

For instance, I remember when I was young, the candy lady who kept the kids at church full of Life Savers. Then there was the man who kept us laughing with all his jokes. There were even the ones who would let us go home with them on Sundays in between church from time to time to hang out and have a break from all the business of the ministry. I can even recall a couple who couldn't have children, and they bought a Nintendo just for us to play with when we came over because we couldn't afford to get one at the time. I remember going to revivals, including tent revivals, singings, benefit singings, weddings, baby dedications, funerals, watchnight services, you name it. Practically anywhere my dad was called to and was needed, we all went as a family most of the time. Even as my siblings and I grew and became school-aged, that didn't stop. We continued to be involved in church activities and were on the go most nights throughout the week.

My mother told me as a young child I would always be known as my father's daughter. That carried a lot of weight to it because I grew up being a daddy's girl. I always wanted to make my daddy proud and not harm his name or his reputation. I still don't want to, and I'm so thankful for all the Lord has done and continues to do through the example of my dad. I could do nothing without the Lord in my life. Oh, I've tried many times to do things my way, but God in His mercy has been right there to correct me and align me right back up with Him and His word. I am so thankful for the love the Heavenly Father has given me through my dad.

My family is dear to me, and I have precious, amazing parents who have always worked well in the ministry together. They love the Lord and have left a legacy everywhere they have been. I'm so proud to say even today they are still in service for the Lord. It is such a blessing, and God knew exactly what He was doing by birthing me into this family to be a part here. But you see, all people saw when I was growing up was how we as a family had it all together and what was portrayed to them. One of my dad's sayings that still to this day rings over and over in my head is, "First impression, lasting impression."

My dad has traits of being very particular about things, how they look and how they are perceived. I guess you could say it's similar to an OCD trait. For example, my dad has always thought highly of a vehicle being clean and staying neat and tidy. When COVID hit and businesses shut down, I knew if my truck was going to be clean, it was going to have to be washed by hand. My dad made a comment one day stating it wasn't that important anymore. His comment really made me stop and think because of the way I grew up knowing my dad has always been particular about things. Just like any family, we have had our ups and downs, our trials and hardships, moments of pain and anger, disagreements, even moments we had to walk away to deal with the issue at hand. Some things have changed, but some things haven't. Some things I couldn't even tell my parents back when I was growing up because of the prominent position they held, and I didn't want to be the one to be blamed for ruining the Lord's ministry or things falling apart. Just like Romans 8:28 states, "We know that all things work together for good." That doesn't mean all we experience in life is good. It does mean, however, that what Satan means for evil, God can use for good. There are things that have left scars and shadows that have haunted me for years. God only knows how many years I have had these scars. Satan loves to keep us focused on our past hurts and feed us lies about how inadequate we are because of them. He likes to tell us we will never measure up, so we just stuff it back—minimizing the situation—put on a happy face, and just keep pretending everything is okay. I was believing the lies that Satan was telling me—how I didn't matter and that it was my parents who mattered. He made me believe that I had to keep making them and the church look good, and everything would be okay. Wrong! This is oh so wrong.

So many times I've heard people say or even had them tell me personally, "If I had only grown up in a preacher's home, a family like yours, then I'd be okay and I wouldn't have all the problems I have today." I've even been told there's no reason why I should be depressed because, "Look at your parents and how you grew up." The fact is, there is no difference in the way Satan attacks a preacher's family than that of any other family. If anything, Satan tries to attack a preacher's family more because of them being in the eyes of everyone. We were always held to a higher standard by others. Oh, the pressures that were put on all of us at times. I can recall being told after I was married that someone had seen my mother in the grocery store, and she was dressed modestly yet not the way they thought she should be dressed, being the preacher's wife. They told her they would never be back to church again because she was out in public dressed the way she was. I'm sure this hurt my mother, but oh how it trickled down and affected me too. I can just about pin the time frame when this happened because I was in elementary school, and the clothes I wore changed from that time on until I was married and out of their house. I can remember my mom telling me, "As long as you do the right thing, others will follow you because your dad's the preacher." Not so.

As a child I was around six years old when I professed to be saved. My youngest brother went forward in a church service, and I followed him. He was only five, but I knew he was the last one in the family other than me not to profess being saved, so I followed him. I didn't want to be the last one to say I wasn't saved. While Dad was there praying with him, I remember just crying and saying, "Jesus, forgive me. Jesus, forgive me," because I didn't want to be left out. I wanted to go to heaven too, but I got up from there still lost as a goose. Where in the world does this saying even come from? I never had a goose, so I'm not sure, but I was lost as lost could be.

I do believe the message that day was on hell. That's one thing we don't hear very much anymore: messages on hell. I can still recall even now the movie we watched growing up called *The Burning Hell*. It would scare me so badly and kept me awake too at times. I remember the movie like I just saw it yesterday.

I even went through the motions of being baptized. Back then the little church my dad was pastoring didn't have a baptistry, so my brother and I were baptized in a creek. Osh! Boy, I can still feel it today, just thinking about how cold it was. I lived life as if I was saved but never felt the drawing of the Holy Spirit until I was fourteen. My teacher at school had been talking to us about salvation, and the Holy Spirit started tugging at my heart. That's when I knew I wasn't saved. It hit me like a ton of bricks that I wasn't going to heaven because I wasn't really saved. I told my parents I needed their prayers and that I was dealing with something but wouldn't tell them what it was.

This went on for around a week, and then our church hosted a candlelight service. It was a Friday night. The visiting lady over it needed someone to fill in for an illustration, so I became one of the five foolish, one of those whose lamp was not lit (Matthew 25:1–13). It still brings me to tears even now as I write "Hallelujah and praise Jesus's holy name." He graciously saved me that night, back in the vestibule of that church. I knew what to do;

it was simple then and still is. How to get saved has not changed. I was already kneeling there waiting for my cue to come out. I believed in Jesus and told God I knew I was a sinner, and I didn't want to go to hell. I asked Him if He would forgive me of my sins and save me so I could go to heaven. I went down the aisle that evening as one of the five foolish for the candlelight service, but knew in my heart for sure I was now saved.

On our way home, I remember thanking my parents for their prayers and told them I had gotten saved. Their reply was simply, "You took care of that when you were young, so you're good." Because of their response (remember, my mother's words— "I will always be known as my father's daughter"—and I didn't want to hinder the ministry nor his reputation), it took me until my daughter was baptized many years later to admit that I too needed to be baptized. I had not done this in the right order because I was baptized after professing to being saved at age six when I really wasn't. God is a God of order, and I wanted to make things right in His eyes (1 Corinthians 4:5). It's not that we have to be baptized to go to heaven. Being baptized is showing others that you have accepted the Lord Jesus as your Savior and now you're making a profession of Him saving you. You are now following in His steps to be baptized, showing others you believe in Jesus and have accepted Him. It was such a blessing, though, because my dad baptized me once again, wanting me to make things right. It brings me so much joy to recall this moment.

Have you accepted Jesus Christ as your Savior? If you have, I want to encourage you to take a few minutes and recall that moment in your life when He saved you and forgave you of your sins—all of them: past, present, and future. Wow! Oh, what a Savior we have that He would take our place and die on the cross for us. I'm so unworthy of what He did, and now that His blood has been applied, God, the Heavenly Father, sees me as worthy, and you too if you've been saved. To recall that moment will encourage you and have you rejoicing and praising His name too. If you haven't been saved, you can be right now as you are reading this little book about why you matter.

God tells us in John 3:16 that He so loved this world that He, **God** gave His one and only Begotten Son, **Jesus**, to die for your sins and my sins. Do you know what *begotten* means? It means to bring into existence by, as if by a parent. God's one and only Son He birthed; that's the only way I can think to explain it. That's how Jesus is God's only begotten. God created us in His image, but Jesus is part of Him in that Jesus is divinely a part of God just like the Holy Spirit is. God loves us so much that He was willing to send Jesus here on earth to shed His blood—His perfect, sinless blood—for us all so that we can be saved and go to heaven. God, in His abundant love for us and His righteousness, knew we could not save ourselves from our sin because of our own unrighteousness. We needed a perfect sacrifice, Jesus, to take our place. So God says "whosoever will," which means you, me, anybody. If we will just accept this truth and believe in Jesus, we can all have eternal life. It's so simple, and yet we make it so hard. It makes me recall a song that I sang as a child. My mother taught it to me. The words go like this: "It's simple as can be. It's clear as ABC. For Christ He came, His life He gave to rescue you and me. Don't wait until you're older. Trust Him it is neigh, and by His grace you'll see His face in G-L-O-R-Y." God loves little children and makes it simple enough for even them to believe in Jesus and be saved.

This world we live in has taken away the simplicity of life from us all. Satan is the ruler of this world, and it is evident all around us. Through life's circumstances, society, different cultures, all the politics, money, and even religions, our thoughts have been so distorted about what is truth. We end up confused about what is and is not the main reason you and I are here and what it means to live life on earth. When you know the truth about Jesus, it will make you free and take the guesswork out of living life here (John 8:32, 36). Just like my dad has said, Satan can use a lake of truth to disguise a pint of poison, meaning it doesn't take a lot to twist the truth. God tells us in His Word, the Bible, His love letter to us, that He will never change (Hebrews 13:8). He is always the same—yesterday, today, and forever more. Our circumstances will change in so many ways, but He never will.

Have you ever just stopped for a moment and thought about how and where God lives out of time? He is not limited by time like we are. Time is a big part of our living here, but it is not to God. Something else that's really awesome about God is He never has to learn anything. God already knows and understands it all—everything! That's so hard for me to wrap my brain around. Think about Peter the disciple, for instance—specifically when he was asked if he knew Jesus (Luke 22:54-62). Right before Jesus was going to be crucified, Peter said he didn't know Him. Not just once but three times in one night before the rooster crowed. Jesus told Peter that he would deny him before it ever happened. Think about it; that means God knew what Peter would do and knew in the nature of that moment even what the rooster would do.

Psalm 147:5 tells us that God's ways and His understanding have no limits and no end. So no matter what you or I do or how we may try, we cannot figure God out. Ever! We will never stop learning about God because He has no end, but our mind has limitations. He has always been and will always be. I don't understand it all, but I know God tells us in Psalm 139 that before He ever made you, He—without the help of Google search—searched you and knew you and understood you better than you could ever know yourself. He even knows how many strands of hair you have on your head (Matthew 10:30). He already has you all figured out. There is nothing you or I can tell Him about ourselves, because He already knows it all. This is where I get so frustrated with myself because of the times I go to others with my problems instead of turning to God, who already knows it all, and talking to Him. Because you know what? The best way for you and me to find ourselves is to go to God and His word. God has all the answers you and I will ever need to live here.

Chapter 3

Shadows

L ooking back through life, I have had shadows that have hindered me, causing pain not just for myself but others as well at times. We all have shadows; you know those things that happen to us in life that are attached no matter where you go or what you do. Shadows can distort our thoughts, our attitudes, and our emotions, affecting our feelings, causing us to act and react in certain ways. Shadows can form because of sin, causing confusion too.

God allows these shadows, not intending to harm us, but He wants to use them to help mold us into Jesus's likeness. It's not that God is the author of the evil behind these shadows because God cannot be evil. Sin is evil, and it is a result of this fallen, sin-sick, cursed world. We all have a sin nature. When God finished creation, which included this world, He said that everything was good (Genesis 1:31). James 1:13 tells us that God doesn't cause confusion. God is not the author of the confusion, and He cannot lie (Titus 1:2).

Sin is not a result of creation, but a result of you and me having a free will to choose. Once Satan approached Eve in the garden with his sly and cunning ways, sin came into existence due to the choices made that day (Genesis

3:14-24). Eve gets a bad rap here. We forget that Adam walked with God in the Garden of Eden before Eve was ever created and Adam was with Eve when she was speaking to Satan (Genesis 2:17, 3:6).

Romans 5:12 tells us that death also came into existence here as well. You see, God is the Alpha and Omega, the Beginning and the End. Nothing brought God into existence, because He always has been and always will be. He already knows all that will happen to each and every one of us because of His sovereignty. I still don't understand this, and it's okay because I don't need to, but I do know that *sovereignty* means God cannot be controlled by anybody. His ways, His rules! No ifs, ands, or buts about it.

God, in His sovereignty, knew and accounted for sin, but it doesn't mean He was the author of it. God did not create us to be robotic so that we would have no choice but to love Him. We have a choice to make. He created us with a free will so that we could choose to love Him. This is just like the shadows in our life: He allows them, but He does not create them. He is right there going through these shadows and circumstances with us. God wants us to become stronger in Him through the circumstances we face, leaning on Him and bringing Him honor, glory, and praise. You see, it's all about how we choose to view them.

We can choose to let these shadows and circumstances consume us, distorting our thoughts about who we really are, or turn them over to God and let Him help us with them. Did you know a shadow forms because something is blocking the source of light? Let's think about the sun for a moment. Depending upon the sun's position, the light can be blocked by an object, causing the shadow to look distorted. The shadow itself can look different from the object because the light is being blocked. It makes me think of a little girl who has just discovered her shadow. She tries to run from it, but she can't. She tries to hide from it, but the shadow follows her. She can't figure out why it's still there, and at times it's even bigger than she is. So the little girl begins to fear it, starting to cry, wanting it to leave her alone. At first, it's cute to her mommy, but then her mommy realizes her little girl is scared of her shadow. The mommy runs with open arms and picks her up to comfort her, explaining that she too has a shadow and there is no need to fear it because it won't harm her.

You see, we all have shadows, and the Heavenly Father wants to do for us what this mommy did for her little girl. He wants us to run into His open arms and let Him comfort us, dispelling all our shadows of life. He loves us all so very much and wants to make our shadows disappear, but He can't when we're holding on to them and allowing them to control our minds. Even though these shadows are attached and causing us pain, Jesus can—and wants to—heal us so they will become smaller and smaller until they don't harm us anymore. If we allow it, Satan will control our thoughts, causing us not to let go of them, and we will lose our focus about who God created us to be. At times we can allow our shadows to become so much bigger than us, and we become fearful, letting them define who we are and cause us to feel like we are not worth Jesus even healing us. These shadows then become self-inflicted and consume us because we refuse to let Jesus have them. Over time we can become bitter and unforgiving.

These shadows can form because of things we go through or things that have been done to us or even said to us. They can have a snowball effect, causing so much harm, because of the way we choose to carry them around and beat ourselves up over them, crippling us. Just like the author and speaker Katherine Wolf says, "We all have our wheelchairs; it's just some are seen and others are not." These shadows are real, they are attached to us, and they can cause havoc if we allow it. In my own life, I have had my thoughts so focused on my own shadows that I allowed them to distort who I really am in Christ. I have let them affect me and infect me. Oh, I've made it look like I had it all together on the outside—you know, "put on a happy face and smile" because no one really wants to see your hurt and pain. I grew up in a preacher's home, and I'm supposed to have it all together. But a lot of times I have allowed these shadows to hinder my walk with the Lord and relationship with others because of the pressures that were put there.

When I was a young child, I went through sexual abuse and allowed it to define me for years, causing heartaches. I turned to food for comfort because I couldn't tell anyone about the sexual abuse going on and gained weight, causing even more insecurities in who I was. The weight gain caused my uncle to start making fun of me, taking away the enjoyment of even going to my grandmother's house for fear he would be there and torment me by his comments and all his crude remarks that I was taking on so personally. I allowed them to cut me to the core of who I thought I was, scarring me so deeply. It was not just the sexual abuse and weight gain, but on top of that, my dad resigning and the moving around to other churches made me unstable in friendships and toward people in general. Oh, I have always loved people and still do, but I never truly became a close friend to most because of the fear of losing them. Generally, girls love friends, and most have the art of gab. I can recall a moment as a young adult when I overheard some women talking about me in the bathroom, not knowing I was in there with them. They were making comments about how I had a problem being and keeping friends. They didn't have a clue about my life and why I had such an issue getting close to people. Another scar with more shadows.

As I got older and started maturing, I can recall going home with a friend and finally getting to lay out in the sun to get a tan. Since it was my first time, I didn't have a clue about how to go about it. I was beat red, burnt to a crisp, by the time we went back to church for the evening service. One of the ladies came up to me and said, "How far does that line go up? I'll bet you're in big trouble when you get home." You see, there are people in all our lives who think they have it all figured out and don't realize the things they are saying can be so judgmental and cut us so deeply. I know I too have been guilty of saying things about others that I shouldn't have when I thought I had it all figured out, causing harm. God is the only one who genuinely knows any of us. I have to admit I don't understand some things I've been through at the hands of other people who call themselves Christians, but I took their actions, their words, and their shunning personally, thinking something was wrong with me and asking myself, "What did I do wrong?" This was especially true of the chastisement and the pressures of having to be different because I was the preacher's daughter. People didn't know me and still don't, but I'm learning it's okay and that I'm okay. God allowed me to go through these things that caused pain, suffering, and shame not to harm me but to form me into what He wants me to be today. Because of the belief system that I was in, though, focused on myself and living life through my feelings, I took it that nobody cared. Nobody wanted to hear about all these shadows distorting my focus and taking it off the bigger picture.

I realize now, it wasn't meant for me to carry these burdens all alone. I love my parents dearly, and all I can think of is honoring them and respecting them, but oh the pressures that were put on our whole family to conform and be held to a higher standard. The shadows that were created affected us all. I have allowed these shadows to distort my thoughts and hinder my walk with the Lord. I learned to care more about what others thought and said than what God said about me. Oh, the pain of it all not being dealt with and just swept under the rug, so to speak. The lies I was believing about myself and others were many. I kept my distance, fearing more things would be said about my family or me that were not true, causing more accusations because people only had part of the story.

The last time my parents moved away to take a church, I will never forget my dad sitting me down and telling me not to feel like I had to defend his name because of what I heard. After my husband was released of all his military duties, we moved back into the area where my dad pastored. I was the only one of my siblings to move back where our family lived, and I heard a lot about what was said about our family. I have felt for years that I couldn't live life to its fullest for fear of what people assumed about us. You know what happens when we assume? It makes a donkey out of you and a donkey out of me, because we cannot be who God created us to be. That's just putting it politely, but its oh so true. Our focus is all on the wrong things. James 3 says we can tame animals, even guide ships, but no one can tame the tongue, and oh what a fire it does kindle. Boy, words sure can hurt others and ourselves at times, but God did not intend it to be this way.

I haven't always handled things correctly, leaning on God like I should. Instead, I became so wrapped up in fear and the distortion of my thoughts, forgetting how God saw me, focusing on how others saw me and intended my life to be lived. I now realize these shadows were not meant to hurt or harm but to help. My focus on them was all wrong.

It took leaving the area where I grew up and God putting me in a church where I was only known for being His child and my husband's wife to redirect my focus. This opened my eyes, my mind, and my thoughts about my scars for these shadows and the truth to be revealed about who I truly am in Christ. Who am I to think I was above anything happening to me in life here? If God didn't spare Jesus, His only begotten Son, from going through things that caused agony, suffering, and shame, then what makes me feel I'm above going through things in life here as well? I'm not comparing what I've been through in my life to what Jesus went through but instead changing my thinking from "I wasn't supposed to have these things happen to me, being who I am" to "Why not me?" Just like our daughter said to me through this bee ordeal when I was laid up for weeks becoming weary at times, asking God what I had done wrong. She said, "Why not you, Mom? We all have it wrong, Mom; we should be asking ourselves 'Why not me?' because we all are sinful people and sometimes good things happen to us."

Isaiah 64:6 says all our righteousness is as filthy rags. We've got it all wrong most of the time about our pain, suffering, and shame. Jesus's suffering on the cross had a purpose. Even through His times of suffering when it was heavy to bear for Him and carry, Jesus purposed "in His heart" to complete what His Heavenly Father intended for Him to complete. Jesus pushed through and saw the joy awaiting Him. That joy was you and me in heaven with Him. This is what Hebrews 12:2 is talking about. Jesus endured the pain and even the shame of the cross so that you and I could be set free. I had so much bondage from the shame, the pain, and the suffering of my past that I allowed it to consume me and control my thoughts, causing me not to be able to live in the present, the here and now. Think—just because Jesus was here as the Son of God does not mean He did not feel pain and suffering like you and I do. He did, and it was heavy for Him at times, but that doesn't mean God wasn't with Him through it all. Jesus is our forerunner in life, and He shows us how to handle these things. He Prayed. Jesus took them to His Father God in prayer. You see, when these things were weighing heavy on me, I didn't follow Jesus's example to carry them to God and let the Heavenly Father help me see things the way He saw them. I carried them myself, allowing what others were saying to affect me, analyze them in my mind, and let my thoughts be my guide. I still prayed—or at least tried to pray—but my heart wasn't in the right place because my mind was so consumed with lies and the burdens.

Do you realize when we pray, no matter what we say to God, He sees our heart? Remember, even though we look at the outside, God sees your and my heart. It's no different when we pray. God sees and He listens to our heart, not our words. God knows if our prayers are honest and if we really mean what we are saying when we pray. These thoughts had become roots of bitterness in me and became strongholds hindering my prayers. The presence of pain in my life did not mean that Jesus was not there with me; it just meant I didn't allow Him to help me with this area of my life. I went pushing on day after day while injured and beaten down on the inside, not letting Him heal me. I was keeping the pain and shame in the hands of those who had hurt me, those who had violated me, those who had said mean and hurtful things about my family, which caused these strongholds. It makes me think of the old saying "Sticks and stones may break my bones, but words will never hurt me."

Words can hurt and they can cut deeply! They can form us in areas we didn't think they could, especially when we let them define us. We all are going through life together, and things can affect us all so differently. We all have different personalities that impact how we act and react to life and how we view things. Some of us take things so personally because of what we have been through. What we go through does affect us, but it doesn't have to control us. God tells us, when these things are controlling us, to bring them to Him and let Him help us carry the load of these moments because it's too heavy for us to carry alone.

Second Corinthians 10:3–4 states you and I are in a battle, and a lot of this occurs in our minds. Once you accept Jesus as your Lord and Savior, He saves your soul and you become more of a target to Satan. Satan hates you, and since he can no longer have your soul, because you gave your heart to Jesus, he will attack your mind to keep you from resting in Jesus and having peace. As long as your mind is focused on Jesus (Isa. 26:3), then you will have peace. Satan doesn't want you or I to have peace. Peace is so attractive to this world, and if the world could just realize the answer to having peace is Jesus, then they would have the freedom they want and need.

We as Christians have the answer, but as long as Satan can keep us consumed with this world, all its cares and woes, then he has you and me right where he wants to keep us: confused, discouraged, and lacking the confidence needed to be all that we can be for Christ. Satan uses life's circumstances to distract us and keep our focus on things that can hinder us. Things such as wars, diseases, injuries, fighting, rumors, finances, drugs, alcohol, sex, and even our own brothers and sisters in Christ. I know people say "Fake it until you make it," but if you are dealing with a stronghold, it's not going to go away until you are willing to face it. I had moments in my life when I did face it and genuinely allowed God to heal me in certain areas, but some of these strongholds were stuffed for so long that I had trigger points causing the hurts and pains to resurface. I would allow thoughts to hinder my daily walk with the Lord, once again affecting me because I wasn't taking them to God as I should have been when they were triggered.

There is no set of rules any of us can follow that will keep us any closer to God. Religions have gotten so in the way of this truth, making us feel as though God loves us more at certain times than others. This is such a lie straight from Satan because he wants us to believe that what we do or say makes God love us more or even love us less. This is not the truth of how it is with God. It's all about our relationship with Him. You see, our sin and our shame can get in the way, hindering our fellowship with Him. That's what was going on in my life through these moments. I was living life through my feelings. I didn't feel loved by God anymore because I felt dirty and ashamed. I wasn't taking it to Him when these trigger moments happened.

The way we grew up, when we did something wrong, we had to rebuild our trust back. I took this so personally because of the effects of my upbringing causing me to think this way about God too. Truth be told, God can never love you any more or any less than He does right now at this very moment. He loves us all no matter what we do; He always has and always will. It's that simple, but we have to do our part when we struggle in life. We must turn to Him, let Him carry our burdens, give it all to Him in prayer and leave it with Him so He can help us. These things that happened in my life were bad and hard to go through, but they were all working for my good to bring God glory. God wants to use these moments to bring out the good in myself and others too.

God knew if I would just allow Him to help me handle these things the correct way, it would make me stronger so I could help others. But I had the thought life of focusing only on the bad and hard times instead of seeing God through them and accepting what He wanted to do with them. God loves for things to be done the right way and in order, and I wasn't doing that. You know it's not just Satan that hinders us at times. There can and are people too who want to keep us ill when we are going through strongholds. People who want to keep you sick in your thought life because their identity is wrapped up in whether you get healing and become set free from your bondage.

My bondage has been no different than anybody else's. I just stayed in church going through the motions even though mine wasn't seen. God really does have it all worked out for each of our lives, every single detail, and he wants it all to be used to honor Him and bring Him praise through it all. The moments we sway can cause pain when we're not focused on Him. What Satan means for evil God does want to turn for good, but we must be willing to allow Him to. During one of these triggered moments, I finally had a breakthrough. I felt trapped with nowhere to hide. God knew just what needed to happen, causing me to say enough is enough. At that moment in time, it didn't seem like that's what He was doing, but He knew what He was doing. I was where I needed to be to break down under the load of all this and let Him ignite me.

Chapter 4

I Can't Do This Anymore

J esus's light finally broke through during this trigger
moment, penetrating the darkness of my mind from all
the years of despair, igniting a spark that caused a flame
to shed light and set me free from this bondage. This roller
coaster of a ride—the ups and downs, the highs and lows,
being controlled by my thoughts at every turn, affecting
my feelings and emotions—was finally coming to an end.
I finally got off this crazy ride of my thoughts.

Do you like roller coasters? I normally do, but emo-
tional roller coasters are different. I was so emotionally
distraught and drained that God was the only one who
could end it and completely heal me. A storm was brewing
yet the Son was beginning to shine, rising on the horizon;
thank you, Jesus. God, in His sovereignty, knew exactly
what storm was needed and the right timing so I would
confront this head-on. You see, not all storms are bad.
Some can be devastating, but when the debris and garbage
are removed, it reveals the hidden beauty underneath.

I've always heard you're either heading into a storm,
going through a storm, or coming out of one. Sometimes
a storm is what's needed to send us spiraling out of control to get to the place where we have longed to be all

along. Have you ever stopped to think a storm could be the answer to your prayers? It may not be the avenue you would have chosen, but God, in His sovereignty, knows what is needed to answer our prayers. I didn't realize it at the time, but this triggered moment is what it took to break me free from these binding chains once and for all. Not just a patch-me-up-and-send-me-on-my-way ordeal like I had other times with God, but the one that would ignite me seeing myself for who I truly am in Christ. This time I gave it all to Him, all that my identity was wrapped up in, all my past hurts, being victimized, my guilt, all the sorrows, the pain and suffering, the false accusations, the blaming game; you name it, and God got it all.

I found out that He can handle it all. He took the lies about my identity I had been wrapped up in and brought me to the end of myself so I could see what He sees: Jesus and only Jesus. The mindset I was living in had short-circuited the true identity I have in Jesus Christ. It short-circuited all that He had done for me on the cross and who I truly am with His blood applied, covering all my sins and wounds. God had a plan all along, but I kept allowing my thoughts to push me back, causing a vicious cycle getting the best of me instead of allowing God to have my best. This triggered moment is what it took to push me to Him so I could live in freedom once and for all. Jesus, in His gentlemanly way, didn't scold me, He didn't judge me for taking so long to understand who I am in Him; He just took me in His loving arms and forgave me, allowing me to lay everything at His feet and tell Him, "I can't do this anymore." I can still see this moment in my life as clearly as I had seen all the pain through these years. God used this moment to start healing my mind and showed me all that I have in being His child, and I will forever be grateful to Him.

There are a lot of people throughout our lifetime who we look up to—such as a superhero, a soldier, or someone who represents a life full of bravery and fearlessness. We all have people like this in our lives. We also want to be brave and fearless, having confidence and being courageous like they do so we too can fight this good fight of life here. I've always said it's so amazing to see what a uniform will do for someone when they put it on. It changes the way they look and the way they carry themselves and how others view them as well. But it's not the uniform that makes the person who they are. It's what the uniform represents when worn. Do you know someone in your life who wears a uniform? Perhaps someone in law enforcement, the medical field, or maybe food service or safety? Maybe you have a uniform of some kind that you wear identifying you as being affiliated with something. There are many different kinds of uniforms in this world, and all serve a purpose of representation. I can guarantee you if you worked for McDonald's today you wouldn't show up wearing a Taco Bell uniform. You probably wouldn't be working there long if they would even let you in. A uniform is something that's of a distinct design put on by someone appointing them to a specific purpose.

I can recall one fall festival we had at one of the churches my dad was pastoring at the time. They allowed the adults to dress up with their children. I didn't have anything to wear, so my dad let me borrow his uniform from the U.S. Army. As I put it on that evening, I didn't quite take to heart the true value of what this uniform represented and stood for: all that my dad had gone through while wearing this uniform in honor of serving our country and protecting us.

I have always loved the uniforms of the military, and when I was young, I wanted to join the military. My family has always been very patriotic, and I wanted to serve my country too, but as I got older, I was told this was no place for a young lady like me. So in my eyes and mind, I was just thrilled to be putting on a uniform, let alone it being my dad's. Not once did I ever think I would have a chance to wear one, making this a very special moment in my life. I don't have the memories of my dad being in the army. That all happened before I was born. I've only seen pictures of my dad in his uniform, but I'm sure when my dad sees his uniform even now hanging in his closet, his heart and memories of it are totally different from mine.

That's the closest image I can think of to relate to what this moment meant for me when I realized how, when I got saved, I put on Jesus's robe of righteousness and that's how God sees me. Because of all the lies Satan had fed me through the years and all the people pressures I'd taken on personally, trying to live up to their standards, I had hindered seeing myself as God sees me. Even though I was saved, I never understood my identity in Christ and what it means to be a true Christian, a true soldier of the cross, a true bondservant for Jesus Christ. I didn't understand that when we accept Jesus as our Savior, we put on a robe of righteousness right along with the garment of salvation (Isaiah 61:10). Through Jesus's righteousness alone are we counted worthy in God's eyes (Romans 3:22; 2 Corinthians 5:21).

You see, I was going through the motions and having emotions all about it, but never understood the true value of what His righteousness meant. Have you ever stopped and taken to heart all Jesus gave up for us? Even what He gave so we could have this robe of righteousness? This robe of righteousness we wear cost Jesus everything He had: His life; His home in heaven, where there is no sin; and coming to earth, where there is sin. Becoming flesh as we are with our human limitations and weaknesses. Coming as a baby here on earth and being born in the lowliest of low, leaving behind His heavenly comforts yet still being without sin. He chose to become a bond slave to carry your and my sins, all the world's sins, and experience death for us. Jesus, bearing the shame you and I deserve, bore our guilt being treated like He was the one who had sinned, yet He was sinless. Jesus knew that being God's Son, it would take His priceless, precious, uncontaminated, sinless blood for our guilt offering so we could be counted worthy in God's eyes. What an honor to put Jesus's robe of righteousness on to be counted as God's child and live free from the bondage of sins and scars (Isaiah 53:2–12).

Because of the mindset I was in, I was taking on a prisoner's uniform conforming me to what I thought I was supposed to be instead of taking to heart who God said I was. Not just a prisoner's uniform like the orange ones you see, but more like the chain-gang stripped ones with all the shackles. I was allowing all these things to affect my identity and bind me down instead of living in the freedoms that I had all along through Jesus's righteousness. God could finally break through and heal me and start working on my thought process.

Even when my husband was stationed in North Dakota, out of concern for our family being up north in the military, the church where my dad was pastoring helped in getting a church started near the air force base. There were no independent Baptist churches in the vicinity there, and to this day the church is still going for Jesus. Even there, once the church got started and we became involved, my identity was still wrapped up in being my earthly father's daughter and not in who I truly am in Christ Jesus. I still struggled with my identity, not realizing that being a Jesus follower was a higher calling than that of being my father's daughter. But God spoke life to me. He showed me who I really am, causing the shadows of my life to start to fade. My circumstances didn't change at that time, but God started working on my heart, opening my spiritual eyes, seeing things as He sees them.

This wasn't just a one-time event where I talked to God, asked for forgiveness, and then moved on. This has been a process, a day-to-day, step-by-step process that God is using in my life. He started changing my mindset. I still have issues and I still have trigger moments, but I'm learning to lean on Jesus as life is happening. I'm not always my best through them either. I've had to ask God and people to forgive me for letting some of them get the best of me. I still say things I shouldn't, and every time I take these moments to Him, in His love and mercy, He doesn't scold me or beat me down; He lovingly embraces me, forgives me, and helps me back up to press on. He keeps me moving forward day by day, one step at a time, trusting Him.

Do you have trigger moments? What is it that triggers you to say things you shouldn't or see things from your past causing you to act and react to certain circumstances? Is it being tired? Is it overeating and feeling guilty? Is it not having enough money to pay bills or buy that certain special something you want? Could it be you being accused of something you didn't do, or you wanted to defend your family and yourself of things being said? Or maybe it's just because you didn't have your caffeine kick for the day, and someone looked at you the wrong way and breathed! We all have triggers at times, some more than others. Just remember, the fact that even though Jesus is with you and is healing you doesn't keep things from still happening. You can learn to lean on Him by trusting Him, and He will help you if you choose to let Him.

Light can always penetrate through darkness, no matter how thick the darkness gets. Think about a candle and how a small flame can light up the place you're in. That's what Jesus is to us here on earth, lighting each step we take. I've still had to face confrontations that couldn't be avoided, but this has all been a part of this healing process. Sometimes I think I need to be muzzled just so I won't react and bite back like a little injured puppy having its leg put back in place after being hit by a car. I claim Psalms 141:3 a lot, for God to set a gate at my mouth to keep my mouth shut and even put a padlock on it. This is a process. God is working on me each and every moment, helping me focus on Him being right there with me. It makes me think of the song our kids and I sang when they were little, but it still applies today. The song is titled, "He's Still Working on Me," and there's a verse that says, "There really ought to be a sign upon my heart. Don't judge me yet cause there's an unfinished part. He loves me as I am, and He helps me when I pray. Remember He's the potter, I'm the clay." I still struggle at times listening to God, but He's teaching me to be more aware of His presence.

God started shining His light, illuminating things, grabbing my attention, and directing me like I have never had happen before. This all worked toward changing my mindset. He started opening my heart to see my true thoughts and feelings. He became more a part of my day-to-day life. One of the most prominent moments during this time was when He started teaching me about using light. That's what is so amazing about God. He will use things in each of our lives as uniquely as we are. He knows what will speak to our heart and get our undivided attention in everyday circumstances. You and I are not just a project to God. He has created each one of us for a purpose here, and our purpose was planned before you or I were ever born. He wants so much to have a close relationship with you and me that He is willing to do what will get our attention.

God used something as simple as a light bulb to teach me more about who I am through Christ and all that I can be. This light bulb kept flickering each morning, still working but not completely connected to the source needed to be most effective. God was using these moments to teach me to stay connected to Him, the source that's needed in my everyday life to shine for Him and let my true identity be known. That way I wouldn't have the time to dwell on the false lies Satan was telling me about myself.

God used the little flashlight on my phone as well. It became the source needed to penetrate through the darkness in the wee hours of the morning getting to where I could spend time with Him, focusing on His presence and not waking anyone else up. He would listen as I talked to Him, and then He would talk ever so gently, guiding me through His word, speaking to my heart while opening my spiritual eyes. I began to see Him and understand more about what it meant for Him to be my Heavenly Father. God had laid it on my heart to pray for prominent people at church and in our community, but now He was teaching me to pray through Ephesians and claim it for my family, myself, and others throughout the world.

During this time, God started using a candle, just one single candle, to show me how much light this one candle flame could illuminate and penetrate through darkness. God started illuminating more of the path I'm on. He helped me to see the differences He could make in my life and the lives of others through this healing process. He used His love letter to focus me and show me how by having my mind set on Him, even though I was just one person, I too could be like this little candle and light up the place He had me in for such a time as this. I could go and reach out to our community and be that light to help them see the true way to Jesus and let Jesus's love shine through me. Then through their healing and coming to know Him, they too could be that shining light to help someone else and be who they were purposed to be. Together we could all reach this world for Jesus.

This was when our pastor started preaching about becoming a warrior. I kid you not—every service we were in, he would mention being a warrior for Jesus. Not just a half-hearted warrior but going all out for Him, putting your whole heart in and being a true warrior for Jesus Christ. For weeks he would mention something in his message about being a warrior, becoming a warrior or being a bond slave for Christ. God started using our pastor's messages to press me. It would be constantly on my heart about becoming a warrior for Jesus. With God working on my heart and healing my wounds, He redirected my focus and changed my mindset to see more clearly who I am in Christ. As it became clearer, I started praying for God to make me a warrior for Him. Remember, as a child, I always wanted to join the military and wear a uniform to show what I stood for in appreciation for our country and those who had fought and died for the freedoms we had.

I've always enjoyed journaling, and at this prominent time in my life, the journal I was using had only a few more blank pages left. Anytime God said something to me, whether it be via a message or His word (his love letter) or a song, even the radio announcer, I would take it and write it down for encouragement and use it to press me forward. Now with this journal almost full, I began asking God if He would give me a journal. You know what? God is right there at all times with you, and He wants to be a part of all the details of your life. He wants our relationship with Him to be the one we're the most in tune with, to include Him and to talk to Him in every detail because He is going through all of life with us.

I love little sayings, such as those things you can read in a few seconds on church signs, in a journal, or even on someone's T-shirt. It wasn't long after asking God for a new journal that we were in a store, and He pointed out one as if to say, "Here you go. Just for you." It was the only one there like it! It was so pretty with its beautiful colors, as if it had been made just for me. Kind of like one of those moments when you're wanting to get that one special gift for that special person in your life, the one you hold so dear to your heart. And then *boom*, there it is. That perfect one-of-a-kind gift you can give them and you know they'll love it because it has *them* written all over it. Well, this was one of those moments, and I knew God did this just for me. On the front of the journal it read, "She believed she was loved & it made her brave." I took this moment so personally—a gift from my Heavenly Father to His daughter.

This little journal, even today, is such an encouragement and blessing to my heart and soul. This reminds me, when we just believe God and take Him at His word, He can do so much in and through each one of our lives. God is a personal God and wants to be personal with us all. He knows just what we all need at every moment of our lives. God started using this little journal to encourage and speak to my heart, and every time I would use it to jot something down. He was showing me things and using words to grab my attention, working on my heart to pull me to Him more each day. With my mindset fixed more on Jesus Christ and knowing I was wearing His robe of righteousness, I became more equipped through Him. I just needed direction on how to become a warrior for Him. I'm afraid I was taken wrong because of having issues with anxiety. Sometimes my anxiety would get the best of me, and I was like a basket case to those around me, especially through my excitement. But God started speaking to me in ways that He knew He could get my attention.

I love music and enjoy singing, especially songs about the love of the Savior. God has used many songs in my life throughout the years, but this time they seemed to be on a deeper level—piercing my heart, bringing life to my soul and my thoughts. God started using the Coke song with the candles that says "I'd like to teach the world to sing in perfect harmony" to speak to me. Then He used the song called "Go Light Your World."

I've always loved nature and being outside. But during this time of falling in love more with Jesus and the relationship with God growing, whenever I went outside, it was as if everything came to life. The trees even became greener and more vibrant in color than ever before. God started showing me where He had put the color green in the Bible throughout scripture. First in the description in Mark 6:39 where Jesus tells the disciples to have the multitude of people sit down on the green grass so they can be fed with the five loaves and two fish. Then in Psalm 23:2 where David talks about God making us lie down in green pastures. This causes my heart to leap for joy every time, bringing a smile to my face just thinking about it.

Have you ever taken a moment to read Psalm 23 and put your name where all the personal pronouns of *I*, *me*, *my*, and *mine* are? I want to encourage you to take the time and do this and see if you too will have a smile and be full of joy before you're done. There is such encouragement in God's word for us all. God even used birds to speak to my heart, whether it be a particular red bird or blue jay, even a woodpecker and geese. The majority of the time it was geese. They would be flying in formation, but sometimes He would show me one flying on its own, looking so lonely and having to work harder to fly by itself.

Have you ever observed geese and the way God created them and why they fly in the formation they do? There's so much we can learn from the way God created them. They are similar to other birds yet so unique, as you and I are, and we can learn from them. Geese flying in a *V* formation create a 70 percent greater flying uplift than flying alone. This increases their capacity to fly greater distances than if they flew by themselves. When the geese fly together, the goose flying at the front gets tired and has to drop back, moving from the point to be behind another goose and rest some from the pressures of being up front. The geese that fly in the back will honk and encourage the ones up front to keep them going, as if to say, "Keep flapping those wings. You've got this. We're still here following you, so don't worry. Keep up the good work! You're doing a great job, and by the way, thank you for all you're doing." Then whenever a goose becomes ill or is wounded, two of the healthy geese will drop down with the ill one and bring support, helping nourish it back to health or bringing comfort until it dies. They together then will fly to where the flock is and join back up with them. If ever a goose tries to drop out of the *V* formation and go on its own, it will instantly feel the pressures of the downward pull and begin to struggle, trying to fly. The goal and route home never changes. It always stays the same. They even teach and train their young ones, teaching them the same route home so they too can be a part of it and join in flying together.

When it comes to living for the Lord, we can learn a lot from the geese. We see unity here and how working hard together pays off through the best interest of others and helping out. By being used in the gifts and talents God has equipped us all with, we too can reach out and be a help to those around us. When we all have the same goal in mind and encourage one another, no matter what each of us is going through, we can be overcomers. Just like Ephesians tells us, we all are a part of the same family, and we should all have the same goal in mind once we become God's children. And last but certainly not least, do you know what the *V* stands for? *Victory.* We can have victory over many things when we all come together and do our part in being God's family. Just like all the geese have a purpose, so do we. We all are here to do what God has purposed us for and can be encouragement to each other during the process of it all. God is so evident in nature and uses so many different kinds of things to get our mindset on Him, His ways, and His love for us.

Even through all the unsettledness of life and all my emotions and feelings, God kept reminding me that He would never leave me or forsake me. He tells us this in Hebrews 13:5. He is present with us through thick and thin, through everything we go through in our life experiences. God started showing me these things from my past were not my enemies to harm me. They were allowed in my life for my good and to bring Him glory through them. He showed me how they were there to help mold me and make me into who He purposed me to be. He meant for these moments to be lessons to learn something about Him, and even now He wants to use them through this healing process to help others.

There was a moment in my childhood when I was blamed for a sexual issue that was going on. Once it all came to a crisis, anger and rage were taken out on me by a prominent adult in my life, even though I was the victim of the circumstance. I couldn't understand at that moment why the anger and rage were directed at me, for I was only a child. I didn't want to have any more confrontations because of fear of being falsely accused. But God, through this time of healing—being an adult now—showed me where the anger and rage came from. This individual was awakened out of a deep sleep, causing this adult to react and handle the situation from a state of being half asleep. There were no questions asked; I was just attacked, and being the child that I was, I couldn't speak up for myself for fear of making things worse. God, in His sovereignty reveals things in His timing when He knows you and I can handle the truth. This is a great example of the fact that somebody's behavior is not always the best indicator of where their heart is. This takes the pressures of being so judgmental about a situation from us.

There are some people who adapt their ways, actions, and responses to avoid pain. Some people will even do their best to dodge a confrontation they want to avoid. There are those too who will tiptoe around others because they lack words to say or because they are afraid they might say something that may be taken the wrong way. No matter the reason, our behavior must be like Christ's, treating others with kindness, care, and concern.

A person can look and act like they have it all together but be drowning on the inside. So many times we keep our attitudes and actions in check but ignore our heart, where the root of our problems really are. Luke 6:45 says we must get rid of the root first, where our stronghold is located, and then that weed in our life will die off. If we don't, it will continue to grow, causing the roots to become so deep, in the dark places of our heart, and take longer to pull out. We must boot the root and guard our heart. Unfortunately, the bad and negative circumstances we go through in life are channeled through our hearts and eventually make it out through our words and actions. We must change the channel like that of TV or something on our computers or phones. When it's affecting us, it's not good for us or those around us. If it's not bringing good things out of us, then we must change it.

I didn't get to this point in my life because of these things happening to me. It was because of the way I carried them around instead of changing the channel and giving them to God when I should have. Because of my choices, they became strongholds. These experiences became my stronghold instead of allowing God to be my stronghold. If I had turned to Him sooner, I could have lived in victory a long time ago. I have to stop here and ask myself, "Does Satan believe more about the potential

I have through Jesus than I do?" How about you? Do you think Satan believes more about your potential than you do? You see, Satan knows he can't have us to destroy us once we become God's children, so he supplies us with daily difficulties, trying his best to defeat us. He tries to keep us in fear and pulled back, staying wrapped up in all our insecurities. Even when our faith in Jesus Christ is not wavering, Satan can keep us discouraged so we won't move forward for Jesus. Satan is already convinced that you and I have power because of Christ and being God's children. That's why he works so hard at keeping us from focusing on God.

Paul tells us in Ephesians 1 about all the blessings we have, the treasures God gives us, and how we are accepted by God. Let that sink in. You and I are accepted by God. God accepts us for who we are because of Jesus's righteousness. We are adopted into His family, and Paul tells us in chapter 6 of Ephesians that we are to take up our weapons of power and pray. We must do this daily. These are not weapons like this world has but weapons that God has for us. We must always remember, anything in this natural world cannot take care of the supernatural battle we face daily. What we can see with our human eye is always being influenced by something we cannot see. Our weapons of warfare are not of this world (2 Corinthians 10:3–6).

This is the most serious battle you and I will ever be in, but God wants to, and can, be our strength through it all. With Jesus in our life, we can say we are fighting in this battle from a win advantage (1 Corinthians 15:51-57). This is the only battle where you and I can say this. These schemes of Satan are real, but as 1 John 4:4 tells us, "Greater is He/Jesus that is in you, than he/Satan that is in this world." I am a firm believer we will all be surprised to see who Satan really is when he is finally revealed to us and how big we have made him out to be. Especially when we just didn't follow God and His way of handling him. Oh yes, Satan's real all right, and the circumstances you and I go through are too, but this is not our final destination (Romans 8:35–39, 2 Corinthians 4:6–18). You and I must have this winning state of mind needed in this battle of good and evil.

Through my desire to have a mindset on Christ and His ways, God started emptying me of myself and changing my way of thinking. He started showing me in Romans 12:1–2, Ephesians 4:1–14, and 2 Corinthians 5:17–21 that with being His child, I needed to change my viewpoint of Him. I needed to change how to live life here and let Him be the one who defined me and not others. These verses tell us to present our bodies a living sacrifice, holy and acceptable to Him, and to become one, with the same goal in mind. Not to be conformed to this world, but allow Him to transform us through changing our mind to be like Christ so that you and I can discern through Him and be found holy, accepted by Him in being His children.

Scientifically speaking, human beings can do something for 21 days to bring on a life change that will be considered a habit. So the way I saw it, for as long as I had been dealing with this destructive and hurtful cycle of insecurities and false identity—some forty-plus years—what was 21 days? Whether trying to stop a destructive cycle or adding something constructive, something meaningful to build life on and help bring healing for myself and others was worth a try. So I started crying out to God for Him to help me change and for Him to empty me. I wasn't necessarily asking Him to change my circumstances but change me and empty me. I asked God to show me what I needed to be emptied of while putting in my life what He wanted instead of what I wanted. He started showing me things I needed to repent of, things I needed to add to my life so I could become who I was in Christ's righteousness. He started changing and conforming my thought life, dealing with what I had been through and how He saw me. He started cleansing me from secret sins, those things I did that I didn't even know were sins to Him, and He was helping me learn to live life to its fullest, alive for Him and others. You see, this was the avenue to God, and He was training me to accept who I was in and through Him.

This reminds me I can have a mindset like Christ and He will make me brave as He is. He hasn't given up on me yet, and He never will, praise be to King Jesus.

While all of this was going on, God gave me a new Bible cover to go with the new journal for encouragement. The front of it says, "Just be who God made you to be." I love seeing it daily because God uses it in my life as a reminder that no matter what I face today, I'm going to be who He has called me to be, and I should let Him handle the rest. I can't do it all. It's not meant for me to, but through His strength, just like Philippians 4:12–13 states, no matter what I'm facing, God will give me what's needed at that moment to go through the day and accomplish what He has for me. I've learned not to worry about tomorrow because it may never come; I just do what He wants me to do today.

God also helped me take on new habits for my mind and my heart. The 21 days turned into a daily process, and I'm learning daily to yield to Him and His voice. Some things are easier to deal with and they bring on a quicker change, but others are taking a lot of prayer and fasting at times due to bitterness and unforgiveness setting in so deeply. I'm learning to be patient in the areas I need to be. This can be such a process for me, waiting on God's timing and not diving into my own because I get so impatient and excited. God is my Father, and I am His child. When we become a child of God, we must remember; just because we are getting older every day does not mean we have arrived with God. We all are different ages in being God's children, no matter how old we are. Some of His children may be seventy years old yet started believing in Jesus as their Savior in their sixties, making them only ten years in age with the Lord. Or vice versa: someone may be only forty years old here but has believed in Jesus since they were ten, making them thirty years old being God's child. That's why it's so important to see each other as God sees us. We all are growing in the Lord at different levels too. We will never be perfect like Jesus is until we are all changed and have a new body like Him (1 Corinthians 15:51–53). God is always taking us from glory to glory, teaching us day by day, called sanctification. Paul talks about this in Romans 6:1–11and 2 Corinthians 3:18. We are going to make mistakes here and say things that hurt or harm each other sometimes, even when we don't mean to. We will not be perfected until Jesus takes us home to heaven to live with Him.

Through this healing process and Jesus shining more vividly in my life, the shadows and darkness started to be depressed and disappear, causing Jesus to be more radiant. My prayer time became more real, and God started directing me on how to pray. He opened my spiritual eyes, allowing me to see some things the way He sees them and to use me for His honor and glory.

I recall a moment when I was feeling like no matter what I did, I just wasn't being as productive for Jesus as I had been. I was praying, asking God to somehow, in some way, please show me He still wanted to use me if He could. He knows when we are being real and sincere with Him. I was feeling low and beat down, like God was so far away and I wasn't sure if He still had a plan for me due to all the failures in my life. Then He opened a door for me to walk through to be used of Him. I didn't know what He was doing at the time until I walked through the door He had opened. Oh, but how God showed up and through His power worked a miracle. I can still see Him pulling me out of this box I had created, proving to me He can use me and wants to.

God works in mysterious ways. I just need to stay in tune with Him daily, focused on Him, so He can. He will use many things in life to keep us focused on Him, His ways, His leading, and His directing. If we're not focused, we'll miss the opportunities He opens up around us daily. It could be a simple gesture such as a smile or a simple "Hello" or even helping someone or being willing to give a hug. Here lately I can't help but think of the difference it has made in my life personally going to the doctor and physical therapy, getting to see each other's faces and their smiles. It's such a blessing to see the pick-me-ups to others when we all smile back and forth, not having to wear a mask. It sure does make these moments in life so much more meaningful for everybody.

Just a few years ago, my husband and I were traveling when the Lord opened up an opportunity for me to be a witness for Him by helping a young lady who was so distraught and in distress. God used this young lady so prominently in my own life to open my heart, eyes, and mind to see that He can still use me.

We had traveled north to go see some of our friends who are like family to us from being in the military together. On this particular trip, we had gone up for a few days to help them with the renovation of their new kitchen and ended up stopping for a restroom break and to grab some ice cream. Once we arrived, I stopped off at the restroom first. All the stalls were taken, so I stood in line waiting my turn. I couldn't help but hear a young lady crying in the stall at the far end. She wasn't just crying softly; she was sobbing loudly and clearly very distraught. While going to the restroom, I couldn't help but think maybe she had been through a miscarriage being there in the restroom and all. I silently started praying for her, knowing how rough a miscarriage is because I too had been through one. What blew my mind was all the people who were coming and going while I was sitting there. They were paying this young lady no mind at all through her distress.

Once I finished and washed my hands, I felt so strongly compelled not to leave without trying to help her. I left the restroom, proceeded to one of the cashiers, and told them of this young lady in the restroom and how I didn't know their policy, but I wanted to see if I could help her. She pointed to the customer service and told me to go to them and have them radio someone from the back to come and help her. After I did this, coming back around the corner from customer service, the young lady had emerged from the restroom still sobbing.

By this time, my eyes met those of the cashier I had spoken to, and she was getting someone to cover for her while I proceeded to come up behind this young lady. I asked her if she was okay and if there was anything I could do to help her. She turned around, and for the first time in my life I didn't see her tattoos, her body piercings, or the way she was dressed; I looked in her eyes and saw her soul. You see, I had already been talking to God about not feeling like He wanted to use me anymore, but God saw my heart and how I was so lost in my identity of who I truly was. I had been talking to the Lord asking Him to open a door for me and show me somehow, some way that He was not finished with me yet. Here was my door, and I didn't even know at the time that this is what He was doing all along. God sees a willing heart and knows when it's ready to be used by Him. God can use you anywhere you are if you're just willing and trust Him.

This young lady, through her tears, said she needed to go to church. At this time, I put my arm around her and explained to her I was from out of town with my husband and we were passing through, but we could take her to church if we knew where one was. The cashier at this time overheard what was being said and proceeded to get her ex-mother-in-law on the phone to come to the store. Once again, the young lady said, "I need to go to church," and she started crying again, sobbing so much it was causing a scene. God told me, "Hug her. Pray out loud in her ear so she can hear you." He said, "Let her know how special she is to Me and how much I love her and how I need her to keep going." So I did. We were standing in the middle of the front isle of the store, but it didn't matter. I knew at that very moment I was standing right where I needed to be.

Once I finished praying, the cashier got a chair and set it between two registers. I led the young lady over to the chair. As she sat down, her head hung down and she was still sobbing. I sat down on the floor in front of her, put my hand on her knee, and looked up at her so I could see her eyes once again. She looked at me and started talking to me, telling me her story. She had five kids and was living with her mom. An old man had picked her up from hitch-hiking and dropped her off to meet a guy to go out of town with for a few days. Her husband had left her, wanting a divorce, because they had a set of babies together and the little boy had died. She was now ready to leave it all behind and go be with their baby boy. My heart sank and I began to cry with her because I realized at that moment this young lady was contemplating ending her life.

She continued to tell me she was praying on the restroom stall floor for God to send her an angel if He was real and she wouldn't commit suicide. She proceeded to tell me how I was her angel. I had a hard time grasping this because of all I had been dealing with in my life personally. This young lady didn't have a clue about what I had been praying for and that she was the answer to my prayers. God saw both of our hearts and both hearts ready for Him. God continued working on us both, and what blew me away is what happened next.

I headed back to the restroom to get some wet tow-elettes, and once I got back, she proceeded to tell us more about her situation with her kids and how she felt they would be better off without her because she hurt so bad in missing her baby boy. She knew her mom could do a better job than she was doing for her kids. While she was explaining this to the cashier and me, the ex-mother-in-law walked up behind her, heard what she was saying through her tears, and put her arm around this young lady's shoulders and broke down with her, sitting down on the plastic bag dispenser. The ex-mother-in-law proceeded to inform her that she couldn't take her life because her children needed her. She then told her that her son was in the military and had taken his life just one year ago, leaving her to take care of the kids he left behind. She told the young lady she could not do that to her mom. At this point we all were crying, seeing what was happening.

Once the young lady was able to walk, we took her to the ex-mother-in-law's vehicle parked right out front, so they could go to church. We exchanged phone numbers and I found out a couple days later that this young lady had spoken with the preacher and she had accepted Jesus as her Savior. I left there that day in tears, praying and thanking God for answering this young lady's prayer. She didn't end her life and He still wanted to use me. What if I had let the lies Satan was feeding me hinder that moment, that moment in her life, and I didn't obey the leading of the Holy Spirit? Where would this young lady be? Remember, when you can't see God's hand, you can trust His heart.

Chapter 5

Living in Freedom

Once I started realizing who I truly am in Christ and what I have in Him through His robe of righteousness, God started breaking me free so that I could be more of who He created me to be. I started seeing Him for who He truly is and who I am with Him. God started showing me Jesus was right there with me all the time while going through the pain, sorrow, shame, and suffering. He started showing me how He sees me with all my scars and wounds. Everything around me started changing. I had been so guilty of putting God in a box, thinking that when He speaks it would be the same way He had spoken to me in the past. God doesn't work that way. God is beyond what my human mind can comprehend (Romans 11:33–36).

I don't know about you, but I like stability in life. I know we have security through Christ. John 10:27–30 tells us we do. But I was putting God in this box, thinking as long as I felt secure, then He was in it. However, this is not so with God. I'm learning when He tells me to do something I'm to do it for Him the best I can. To do this, I have to stop trying to be such a people pleaser. This doesn't mean I am to be rude or disrespectful to others, but God sees my whole life. He has a purpose just for me, and He does for you as well. God even wants us to do it when we're scared, just like Moses did in obeying Him when he picked up the snake by the tail (Exodus 4:3). Wouldn't you be scared? God knows what He wants to do in and through each of our lives for such a time as this. When God says wait, be willing to wait. Don't try to go ahead of Him, because you can't. He's God, and neither you nor I can stop His timing or change His plans. Be willing to go through the process, the step-by-step, moment-by-moment, and day-by-day tasks. No matter what others may say or think, we are to obey God. Everything we do is to be done for God and God alone. We are to bring Him honor and glory while helping others and not do things for man's approval.

It's not just about what's on our minds and in our thoughts. Isaiah 55:8–9 tells us God's ways and thoughts are out of this world compared to any of ours. God wants to turn our mindset to living here with His kingdom in view. God created you and I for different reasons. We all have similarities, but we are all uniquely, individually designed by God here for a purpose. God has a plan for each and every day of your life here to be who He created you to be—right here, right now, in the present, being alive and glowing for Jesus (Matthew 5:14–16). So don't hit repeat! Each and every day is a new day (Psalms 118:24), and it's all about Jesus.

No matter what has happened in your life, He wants to use it all—your ups, your downs, your heartaches, your physical impairments, even all your imperfections. Remember, He's still working on you and me. We're all misfits, perfectly imperfect, and God wants to use what makes us who we are and use it all to bring Him honor and glory. Do you think that during the times when you were not living for Him throughout your life, He didn't know what He was getting when He chose you? God loves you oh so dearly, and I can't express that enough. You are priceless to Him. In Psalms 139:16 He says before you were ever born, He had a plan and purpose for your life. God created you, and there is nothing you can do to surprise Him that He doesn't already know. Even through all our weaknesses and mess-ups, He still loves us, accepts us, and wants us to represent Him being the light this world needs, shining ever so brightly, so they too can see their need for Jesus. God is our Creator, and we all are made in His image (Genesis 1:26–27).

This makes me think back to when I used to do cakes for a ministry to help others save money and just charge them for the supplies needed. Our family was in an accident, causing some vertebra and pinched nerve damage, so now I don't get to do them as often. But during this time of decorating cakes, God laid it on my heart through my mother's comment to use these moments to pray for those I was making the cakes for. God blessed me with the gift of being creative through taking home economics class my sophomore year of high school and was introduced to cake decorating there. This became such a blessing, saving us all money. As I was learning to stack cakes for weddings and celebrations, I offered to make my dad's fiftieth birthday cake for the church-wide celebration. With my dad being such a patriot for our country and fascinated with eagles, I wanted to do something around this theme. It's awesome to see how God has given my dad some messages to preach about the eagles seen in scripture. Come to think of it, dad's life verse is Isaiah 40:31: "But they that wait upon the Lord shall renew their strength; they shall mount up with wings as eagles; they shall run, and not be weary; they shall walk, and not faint." Hallelujah. What a great reminder for me.

Do you have a life verse? One that you claim and cling to? I'm not talking about one you're familiar with. If you're like me, you have more than just one you really like and you're drawn to. But I'm talking about that one verse, the one you claim and God uses it in your day-to-day life to live by. I would have to say mine is Colossians 3:17: "And whatsoever ye do in word or deed, do all in the name of the Lord Jesus, giving thanks to God and the Father by Him." This is such an encouragement for me, and I want to encourage you, if you don't have a life verse, talk to God and He will direct you and give you one too. Try to memorize it and claim it to live by. It will encourage you and you'll be amazed how God will use it and bring it to your heart and mind during times you need it.

Back to my cake story. I knew I needed to fix a large cake to feed everyone at church, and knowing how my dad loves eagles so much and knowing his life verse, I wanted to put an eagle on top of his cake. Not just as a topper, but one He could eat. My dad loves chocolate and God gave me the idea of using a chocolate Easter bunny. You know those hollow ones? I found one and piped an eagle on it. To see the picture even now, people still can't believe the eagle was made from a bunny. You see, I knew the eagle started off being a chocolate bunny, but no one else did until I told them. It's the same way with God. He created you, so He knows you and what you are made of. God knows your strengths, your weaknesses, even your hang-ups. He knows what makes you tick and how you think even better than you know yourself. God has all the answers you'll ever need to live here on this earth. It is so important for us to see things through His eyes and have Christ's mindset. Not just in the areas we want to but in our whole thought process. Acts 17:28 tells us in Him we live, move, and breath. This means God, in His sovereignty, gives you and me the health we need to keep moving and the oxygen needed to breath, or we wouldn't be here moving at this very moment. We all have a story to tell. God allows things in your life so specifically unique for you, just like He has and does in mine.

God wants you to use your unique, special circumstances and situations to tell others what He can do and what He wants to do for them too. Recall what God has brought you through to bring you to this point in your life and help you deal with what He's doing in your life today. This will bring encouragement and will help push you forward into your purpose. Think of Jonah; God prepared a great fish to swallow Jonah for that particular moment in time when the fish was needed (Jonah 1:17). And Sarah—look at how God brought life out of her old, dead womb (Genesis 18:12–14). How about the little widow who only had a clay jar of oil, yet God, in His sovereignty, multiplied it, saving her two sons, paid her bills, and gave her money to live on (2 Kings 4:1–7). And the list goes on and on. That's the God you and I serve, and He wants to use all our life stories to bring Him praise and glory.

My husband has always wanted land for as long as I've known him. We've always had it on our bucket list to build a cabin together, and he wanted land to go with it. As the years went by, we would change our plans, downsizing them to what we needed for the moment. God had a plan all along for us to build, but it just wasn't His timing yet. God started working on our hearts a few years back. My husband wanted more land, and my heart saw more the need to be closer to my parents to help take care of them, with them being older now. Through praying, we both started feeling the pull to be in a location closer to our jobs and to my parents. God had the perfect place picked out for us that far exceeded our prayers and even gave us some of our wants too. That's just like our Heavenly Father. Ephesians 3:20 says God can do far above and beyond all that we could ever imagine.

I'm telling my age here, but do you remember the cartoon from the 1970s about the little boy who could summons a gigantic robot by the name of "Gigantor"? I hardly remembered it myself, but God used it in such a powerful way one morning when I was reading in Ephesians 3:17–21. Having had brothers, and being the only girl, I'm sure we watched it, but God pressed on me to look up the theme song on YouTube. He used it to give me a visual of how He can do far above and beyond all that we could ever imagine. The theme of "Gigantor" says he's "Bigger than big, taller than tall, quicker than quick, stronger than strong, ready to fight for the right against wrong." You see, God's power is in us, through the Holy Spirit's leading, and we can stand in His strength. God can work through us. When we are trusting in Him, we have the power needed to fight this war of good and evil. God just wants us to do things His way by obeying Him and letting Him work through us. Long story short, God opened doors and gave my husband the land he wanted and a foundation for us to build a little cabin. I had already moved thirteen times through growing up in a preacher's home, marrying, and moving around with my husband in the military, and I'm praying this will be my final move here until I go home to live permanently in heaven with Jesus. Hallelujah, and I won't be carrying anything with me for that move because

I won't need anything. Have you ever moved before? All the stresses, all the decisions to be made, and all the hard work involved. It takes a toll on you and your family, fur babies included, no matter your age. It can be exciting, but wow, it's hard work and hard to stay above the stress of it all. Through God's working, He opened the doors and gave us a place to call home. So we're here now in this location for such a time as this.

God has a plan for all of us, and through His faithful love He directs us to where we are needed and where He wants to use us. On top of this, God, in His sovereignty, even worked it out for my parents to be so close that they are now our neighbors. The Lord sold their home within just a few days as COVID hit and we all pitched in to move Mother and Dad in with us. They lived with us for nine months through the building process of their log cabin. We stored their things in a little building they purchased and our basement and did the best we could through the circumstances. Boy, what memories we have through that season of life. My parents spent a lot of time on our big wrap-around porch during the COVID season with my husband coming home to work due to his office shutting down. Then the moment my dad almost got shot trying to kill a copper head coming in after dark, and God allowing his gun to jam. All the times my dad and I would be up in the wee hours of the morning, each of us in our own little areas, quietly spending time with God. Even now there are times I get up early and look across the way to see the light on in my precious daddy's study, knowing He too is spending time with our Heavenly Father and having fellowship with Him. It still brings tears to my eyes recalling those moments, but it was through all these unsettled times God was working a miracle in this heart of mine, igniting a spark and bringing healing to my thoughts about life and dealing with this identity crisis. God used these all as teachable moments to begin training me to become His Daughter of VALOR.

Since surrendering to God and giving Him everything through my false identity and now aligning with Him about living life here and all the plans He has uniquely just for me, He has started teaching me and training me more about who I truly am in Jesus with His robe of righteousness on. God, through His sovereignty, tells me I'm worthy and He wants me to be the daughter of VALOR, He created me to be. He guides me through the Holy Spirit and directs me while telling me to lean on Him and not people because He is the One there with me daily.

Through God's leading, I am learning to put His whole armor on daily and be thankful that I am here and that I get to be a light for Jesus. He tells me to shine daily and bring Him into every situation I am in for that moment. Jesus is present with me, and through the power of the Holy Spirit, He is teaching me not to worry about my past, but be like a stream flowing and don't pass over the same pebble twice; just keep moving forward. I'm not to even worry about tomorrow, because He has already taken care of it, walking ahead of me there. I'm not promised a tomorrow. I am learning this is a daily process, a step-by-step, moment-by-moment, here-a-little-there-a-little process. I am not to try to control God or the outcome to make something happen, because He has a timing for everything. I am to live in this moment, one day at a time, knowing that through His sovereignty He's got me, and this whole world. He will handle all that concerns me, whether it be family, church, community, or this world. I am to be the light He needs me to be in the here and now and let Him direct every step I take. I cannot jump ahead of Him no matter how hard I push because God has already been there, literally ahead of me, and I can trust Him.

Through this recent bee injury that caused my life to come to a halting stop, God used this time to heal me in more ways than I thought possible. God sees my heart, and a few weeks before this happened, He gave me Psalms 28:7 so personally to claim. Little did I know the reason why, but He knew. He impressed on me to memorize it to be encouraged and claim it through this time in my life of physical pain and suffering. Psalms 28:7 tells me, "The LORD is My strength and My shield, My heart trusted in Him, and I am helped: Therefore, My heart greatly rejoiceth; and with My song will I praise Him."

Through all the months of trying to heal correctly, doing what the doctor said, and my husband's encouraging me to stay put trying to avoid more surgery and prayerfully keep my foot, I learned that there are times God calls us to stay down and relax because He has a plan even through our sufferings.

I have to stop here and thank God's precious Son, Jesus, my groom, for what He did for me through His pain and suffering by taking my place on the cross for my sins. That is something I could never have done. Even if I tried to, it never would have made a difference like Jesus's blood did. You know Jesus could have called ten thousand angels to rescue Him, but He chose not to (Matthew 26:53–54). Why? Because according to Hebrews 12:1–3, we see it was because of what Jesus saw before Him, the joy that was coming. That joy was you and me in heaven with Him.

I learned more about staying disciplined in prayer and the Holy Spirit teaching me to endure through learning to walk again. Through this process, by the Holy Spirit's leading, He taught me how God's love letter, the Bible, is the spiritual therapy for my soul to walk by daily. Physical therapy is used to stay focused on targeting those areas where muscles, tendons, and ligaments need to be restored to move in life and function with the rest of our body. It's the same way with getting in God's love letter to us in our life personally here. It's His therapy to live life here alive. Get that: *alive*. Living life here to its fullest and having the mindset like Christ.

God never gave up on me, and He gave me the time needed to learn more about myself and opened a pathway for me to become a part of Life on Fire, a faith-based movement, teaching me and helping me to see more of my potential. God used this movement to encourage me and help me learn how to get moving and let Jesus shine through my story for His glory. Through this gift God has given of becoming a Daughter of VALOR, God opened the door to partner with Jesus in writing this book. Jesus has lead and guided me through the Holy Spirit, recalling what God has done for me and let you know how very special you are to Him. He also wants you to become His daughter of VALOR too. God wants you to live aligned with Him living out your royalty. He wants to change your perspective of how you view life here and set your mind to be like Christ's bringing Him honor through your uniqueness and through your life story. There is someone out there who needs to hear your story. God can use it in their life to make a difference for Him. He wants you to come to the realization of why you matter and that you too are a piece of this big puzzle here called life. It doesn't matter how old you are. God wants you to live your life as an overcomer and willing to let Him be your conqueror.

As we know, there is a problem in this world, and by staying in this frame of mind that's set on Christ Jesus, we have the solution to the problem. This world wants freedom to live in, but they are going about it so blindly. Jesus is the only answer to their blindness, and we have the answer they need. By shining our lives for Jesus in our communities, our realm of influence, this world can see the way to have true freedom. When you and I are aligned with Jesus—not just by being someone who sits on the sidelines cheering Him on, but by joining in together, aligned with Him in unity; working together using our talents, gifts, and interests; allowing Him to be our source needed—we can be the beacon this world needs. Just like that of a lighthouse, shining on the shores of the coastline, letting its light shine for those weary, tired, and worn-out travelers who are stuck in harm's way. We are to be the light for those who are being tossed back-and-forth, back-and-forth, unsettled in this world, in need of direction, and in need of a way to safety, peace, and freedom.

We have the power through Jesus, His robe of righteousness and the leading of the Holy Spirit to help others see the truth and the way to live life here. We can shine just like those who have come before us; such as Moses, Abraham, Isaac, Ruth, Esther, the disciples, and Paul. Even those we have known throughout our lifetime too. You and I have this same power in us to be brave and courageous just like they were, to be a warrior ready to stand tall for Jesus, lighting this world up for Him. We all can live life alive and be overcomers. We are God's children, a part of His royal family, and can live a victorious life here in our royalty of who we truly are for His purpose in the here and now, doing our part for our Heavenly Father's kingdom. By living as God's Daughters of VALOR, you and I can be the light needed in this world to turn others to safety, showing them that Jesus truly is who He says He is—the only way, the truth, and the life—and go live in heaven with Him. We can be the difference we want to see in others by letting it start with you and me. This is a simple process, but remember it is a process living each and every day in the moment.

The first thing you must do is surrender. Surrender to the fact that Jesus is the only way and that He truly wants to be your Commander and King. You must focus and know that He is present with you at all times to direct you. He will make you brave like He is so you too can live in freedom. You can live free from your bondage of past hurts, addictions, hang-ups, and anything you have in your life at this moment. Jesus can heal you from it all when you surrender to Him. Put your confidence in Him and trust Him. Your identity in Him is far greater than any other identity or label you have here on earth. Your identity in Him will last forever. Through believing and trusting Jesus, you will see yourself for who you truly are with Him. Accepting Jesus, who brings you worth, will cause you to accept yourself for who God has created you to be, making you braver than you ever could imagine. Through Jesus, you too will see yourself in right standing before God in what Jesus has done on the cross, which cleanses you from your sins. Through His robe of righteousness, you will be made brave and can be God's Daughter of VALOR, a Victor Aligned Living Out Royalty.

Chapter 6

A Strategic Plan

Through the process of the Lord opening my heart to be receptive to His will and His training, He has shown me how to become God's Daughter of VALOR, to be the warrior He created me to be. He has given me a strategic plan that works even when life is overwhelming me. It is an intentional plan that works in those moments when Satan tries his best to throw us off course, causing us to live life as POWs here under his influence in our thought process instead of living with a Christ-centered mindset in victory. My prayer for you is that Jesus will help you through this strategic plan to be God's Daughter of VALOR with Jesus as your Commanding King and not to be just a cheerleader on the sidelines cheering Jesus on.

First, you must choose to surrender. Accept Jesus for who He truly is and be all He wants you to be. Let Him be your Commanding King. Stop being a prisoner of war in your thoughts, running your life based on your feelings and emotions. Grab hold of all the power you have through Christ wearing His robe of righteousness. Be all He has created you to be for this moment. You are worthy of living for Him and all He has done for you. Realize you are a part of *the* royal family, honor Jesus's name, and represent God well. Abandon the need to control what others think about you, give up your self-protective stance, and accept your identity through Christ. Believe in the unique you that you are. You are the only one in this world like you, so be joyful in being yourself. All of God's children put their uniform, Jesus's robe of righteousness, on the same way, and none of us are better than the others. Always remember, God doesn't make mistakes. He never says "Oops" or "Uh-oh"! You are created for this moment in time. You are needed here and can live in victory while you're here. God has you in His hand, and nothing is going to happen to you that He can't control through His Sovereignty.

When you surrender, you are no longer a POW. It's time now to suit up to be His warrior. Suiting up is needed daily to live victoriously and be all God created you to be. You must remember, the power you need for this battle comes only through God's weapons. Ephesians 6:10–18 says you are able to live here in the power of our Commanding King by putting His complete armor on and standing in His weapons needed for this spiritual war. This battle here is between good and evil, light and darkness, against the powers and principalities of this atmosphere. Remember, there is always something you can't see controlling what you can see. God's armor of power is the only way you can stand against these evil forces that are really there. It won't stop them from raging, but God's armor will keep you from being overthrown and defeated. Every piece of armor is important and is needed for this battle. Remember you are covered in Christ's victory garment, but you need God's armor to stand in His strength that comes through staying in close fellowship through prayer and thanking Him.

Our Commanding King is always present, always awake, and always alert. So talk to Him all the time at any time. He will direct you through the guiding of the Holy Spirit as you partner with Him daily in this battle. Our sword is His word, your love letter from Him to you personally. Use it to train by and learn line-upon-line, precept-upon-precept, here-a-little and there-a-little. He will give you what you need for each moment of everyday life. Remember, God is everywhere. He has already walked ahead of you and prepared your way and knows what you need for each moment.

Now, stand for Jesus. You have what is needed for this battle. Stand-up in Christ's righteousness ready for your daily duties. You are suited now for the moment. God is not just sovereign, He is also providential, meaning He can take care of anything that is in your life and in the way of what He wants to accomplish in and through you. Stay in this moment and stand in His strength; not your own. You have gotten to this point in your life because you have chosen not to let your wounds infect you and not be identified by them. You have chosen to let God use you because of your scars and wounds and be identified in Jesus who is your true identity. This choice of faith comes by knowing you are useful to God in battle here. He can use your scars to bring Him honor and praise as you take a stand for Him.

Show-up and be counted present. You are created for a purpose here for God's Kingdom. Show-up, be accounted for, and be ready to be all God created you to be in your field of impact. Be an encouragement to others and help them. God gave you talents and gifts that He wants you to use for Him. This brings you joy through the process as you share them with others, helping them and bringing them joy as well. Show-up and do your best for Him every day. God doesn't expect you to have all the answers; He just wants you to show-up and live life to its fullest knowing Jesus, your Commanding King, is with you step-by-step, moment-by-moment, every second of every day.

Now shine! Shine for Jesus. Just like a candle shining the way in this dark and stormy world. Embrace who you are in Christ. Be God's Daughter of VALOR, living out your royalty by being who He created you to be. Be-the-link and do your part in His royal family. Let your identity in Christ Jesus be how you operate in your line of work here and be all you are created to be for this moment in time. You are a unique piece to this big unit here, this puzzle called life, and you do matter. You can stand in the power you have in the Lord and be the light He needs you to be for those around you. Let your Commanding King train you to be brave and courageous and be who God has purposed you to be. Share your unique story, cross those bridges, and turn them into merit badges, crowns to bring our Heavenly Father glory through them all. Let God use your scars and pains of life here to help others. Those who are still wounded and in need of someone to be their light to help them get to the source, Jesus, the only true light needed, to bring complete healing and recovery. God's love can shine through you showing this world there is nothing impossible for Him. With God, He can make them possible too just as He has you. Through God, all things become possible for you to be the Daughter of VALOR you really want to be, living in the royalty only made possible through Jesus's love and grace. So go, shine for Jesus in your field of impact. Bring the light needed to this world here by being the unique you God created you to be, because *you* really do matter.

CPSIA information can be obtained
at www.ICGtesting.com
Printed in the USA
LVHW021632191122
733280LV00028B/2195